# THE FIRSTBORN

# THE
# FIRSTBORN

## Laurie Lee

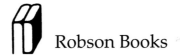
Robson Books

This edition published in Great Britain in 1997 by Robson Books,
10 Blenheim Court, Brewery Road, London N7 9NT

A member of the Chrysalis Group plc

First published in Great Britain in 1964 by Hogarth Press

Copyright © 1963 Laurie Lee
The right of Laurie Lee to be identified as the author of this work
has been asserted by him in accordance with the Copyright,
Designs and Patents Act 1988

**British Library Cataloguing in Publication Data**
A catalogue record for this title is available from the British Library

ISBN 1 86105 101 8

Printed in Great Britain by St Edmundsbury Press Ltd, Bury St
Edmunds, Suffolk

To Jesse's Mother

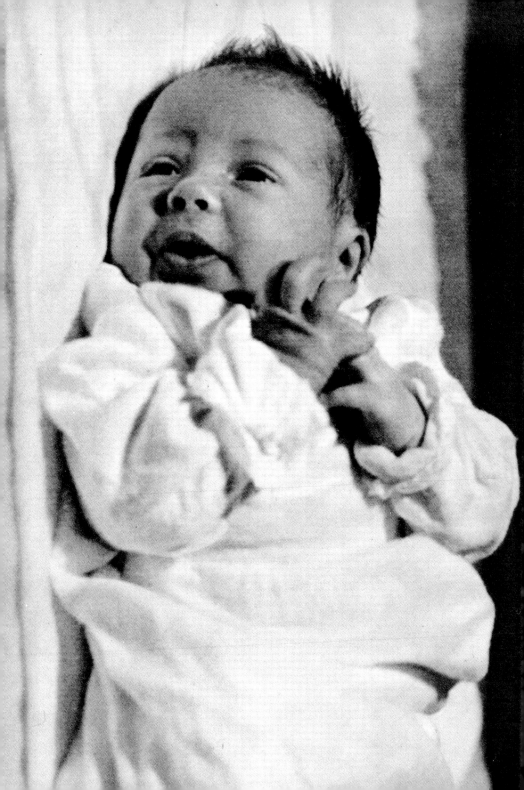

She was born in the autumn and was a late fall in my life, and lay purple and dented like a little bruised plum, as though she'd been lightly trodden in the grass and forgotten.

Then the nurse lifted her up and she came suddenly alive, her bent legs kicking crabwise, and her first living gesture was a thin wringing of the hands accompanied by a far-out Hebridean lament.

This moment of meeting seemed to be a birthtime for both of us; her first and my second life. Nothing, I knew, would be the same again, and I think I was reasonably shaken. I peered intently at her, looking for familiar signs, but she was convulsed as an Aztec idol. Was this really my daughter, this purple concentration of anguish, this blind and protesting dwarf?

Then they handed her to me, stiff and howling, and I held her for the first time and kissed her, and she went still and quiet as though by instinctive guile, and I was instantly enslaved by her flattery of my powers.

Only a few brief weeks have passed since that day, but already I've felt all the obvious astonishments. New-born, of course, she looked already a centenarian,

tottering on the brink of an old crone's grave, exhausted, shrunken, bald as Voltaire, mopping, mowing, and twisting wrinkled claws in speechless spasms of querulous doom.

But with each day of survival she has grown younger and fatter, her face filling, drawing on life, every breath of real air healing the birth-death stain she had worn so witheringly at the beginning.

Now this girl, my child, this parcel of will and warmth, fills the cottage with her obsessive purpose. The rhythmic tides of her sleeping and feeding spaciously measure the days and nights. Her frail self-absorption is a commanding presence, her helplessness strong as a rock, so that I find myself listening even to her silences as though some great engine was purring upstairs.

When awake, and not feeding, she snorts and gobbles, dryly, like a ruminative jackdaw, or strains and groans and waves her hands about as though casting invisible nets.

When I watch her at this I see her hauling in life, groping fiercely with every limb and muscle, working blind at a task no one can properly share, in a darkness where she is still alone.

She is of course just an ordinary miracle, but is also the particular late wonder of my life. So each night I take her to bed like a book and lie close and study her. Her dark blue eyes stare straight into mine, but

off-centre, not seeing me.

Such moments could be the best we shall ever know – these midnights of mutual blindness. Already, I suppose, I should be afraid for her future, but I am more concerned with mine.

I am fearing perhaps her first acute recognition, her first questions, the first man she makes of me. But for the moment I'm safe; she stares idly through me, at the pillow, at the light on the wall, and each is a shadow of purely nominal value and she prefers neither one to the other . . .

Meanwhile as I study her I find her early strangeness insidiously claiming a family face.

Here she is then, my daughter, here, alive, the one I must possess and guard. A year ago this space was empty, not even a hope of her was in it. Now she's here, brand new, with our name upon her: and no one will call in the night to reclaim her.

She is here for good, her life stretching before us, twenty-odd years wrapped up in that bundle; she will grow, learn to totter, to run in the garden, run back, and call this place home.

Or will she? Looking at those weaving hands and complicated ears, the fit of the skin round that delicate body, I can't indulge in the neurosis of imagining all this to be merely a receptacle for Strontium 90. The forces within her seem much too powerful to submit to a blanket death of that kind.

But she could, even so, be a victim of chance; all those quick lively tendrils seem so vulnerable to their own recklessness – surely she'll fall on the fire, or roll down some crevice, or kick herself out of the window?

I realise I'm succumbing to the occupational disease, the father-jitters or new-parenthood-shakes, expressed in: 'Hark, the child's screaming, she must be dying.' Or, 'She's so quiet, d'you think she's dead?'

As it is, my daughter is so new to me still that I can't yet leave her alone. I have to keep on digging her out of her sleep to make sure that she's really alive.

She is a time-killing lump, her face a sheaf of masks which she shuffles through aimlessly. One by one she reveals them, while I watch eerie rehearsals of those emotions she will one day need; random, out-of-sequence but already exact, automatic but strangely knowing – a quick pucker of fury, a puff of ho-hum boredom, a beaming after-dinner smile, perplexity, slyness, a sudden wrinkling of grief, pop-eyed interest, and fat-lipped love.

It is little more than a month since I was handed this living heap of expectations, and I can feel nothing but simple awe.

What have I got exactly? And what am I going to do with her? And what for that matter will she do with me?

I have got a daughter, whose life is already separate from mine, whose will already follows its own directions, and who has quickly corrected my woolly preconceptions

of her by being something remorselessly different. She is the child of herself and will be what she is. I am merely the keeper of her temporary helplessness.

Even so, with luck, she can alter me; indeed, is doing so now. At this stage in my life she will give me more than she gets, and may even later become *my* keeper.

But if I could teach her anything at all – by unloading upon her some of the ill-tied parcels of my years – I'd like it to be acceptance and a holy relish for life. To accept with gladness the fact of being a woman – when she'll find all nature to be on her side.

If pretty, to thank God and enjoy her luck and not start beefing about being loved for her mind. To be willing to give pleasure without feeling loss of face, to prefer charm to the vanity of aggression, and not to deliver her powers and mysteries into the opposite camp by wishing to compete with men.

In this way, I believe – though some of her sisters may disapprove – she might know some happiness and also spread some around.

And as a brief tenant of this precious and irreplaceable world, I'd ask her to preserve life both in herself and others. To prefer always Societies for Propagation and Promotion rather than those for the Abolition or Prevention of.

Never to persecute others for the sins hidden in herself, nor to seek justice in terms of vengeance; to avoid like a plague all acts of mob-righteousness; to take cover whenever flags start flying; and to accept her faults and frustrations as her own personal burden, and not to blame them too often, if she can possibly help it, on young or old, whites or coloureds, East, West, Jews, Gentiles, Television, Bingo, Trades Unions, the City, school-milk, or the British Railways.

For the rest, may she be my own salvation, for any man's child is his second chance. In this role I see her leading me back to my beginnings, reopening rooms I'd locked and forgotten, stirring the dust in my mind by asking the big questions – as any child can do.

But in my case, perhaps, just not too late; she persuades me there may yet be time, that with her, my tardy but bright-eyed pathfinder, I may return to that wood which long ago I fled from, but which together we may now enter and know.